This book was inspired by the work of Sol LeWitt. I first became intrigued by LeWitt's art after visiting his work at MassMOCA, the Massachusetts Museum of Contemporary Art, in North Adams, MA. The museum houses an incredibly rich and large exhibit of LeWitt's wall drawings. At the time, I was teaching 7th and 8th grade math in New Haven, CT's public schools. I began to incorporate LeWitt's techniques into my math curriculum. The results were exciting and immensely rewarding. I called my project "Teaching Math Through the Art of Sol LeWitt." I eventually left my job as a full-time teacher to work as a teaching artist, bringing this same concept to children in schools all over the Northeast – including lessons for 3rd graders through high school students. You can see more examples of my work in education on my web site – www.bethklingher.com.

I would like to thank Jaclynn Hart, Programming Director of Hartford Performs, and Larisa Kottke, Grants and Office Manager at Hartford Performs, for giving me the idea to create a coloring book. Without their encouragement and enthusiasm, I never would have embarked on this project. I would also like to thank the numerous friends and colleagues who spent hours and hours coloring and trying out each project. And lastly, I would like to thank my husband, Reid Lifset, my favorite cheerleader and supporter.

2

Table of Contents

4

Introduction

Who was Sol LeWitt and Why Use His Art for a Coloring Book?

Sol Lewitt was a Connecticut artist famous for a series of abstract wall drawings based on his theory of Conceptual Art. Like the composer of a musical score, LeWitt wrote the instructions for his paintings and let others, often trained draftsmen, actually create the paintings. Although these draftsmen followed LeWitt's instructions, there was often room for them to add their own creativity and interpretations, creating unique works of art each time the pictures are created.

What Do the Instructions Look Like?

Sol LeWitt's instructions varied from very simple, straightforward directions, to less detailed, more general instructions that required the drafter to make many of their own decisions. Here is an example:

A square divided horizontally and vertically into four equal parts, one gray, one yellow, one red and one blue with color and India ink washes.

How Can We Use the Instructions to Make Art?

This coloring book does not use LeWitt's specific instructions; rather, I have created my own instructions that are inspired by LeWitt's wall drawings. His abstract art contains geometric shapes, repeating patterns, and combinations of simple lines that create interesting and complex designs – perfect for coloring, or creating your own art.

How to Use this Book?

This book contains a number of designs that can be colored as is – just like any other coloring book. However, for those of you who would like to follow the instructions and interpret them yourself, I have included additional instructions for you to follow. In this case, you should feel free to follow the instructions, as you like. Feel free to interpret, revise or change them to add your own personal touch.

I encourage you to share your finished work and any instructions you write on our facebook page – Sol LeWitt Inspired Coloring Book or via the hashtag #ColorLewitt.

.

Geometric Drawings

Please enjoy coloring the following drawings using colored pencils, markers or other media. It may also help to have a ruler on hand for some of the lines. You're welcome to work free hand too – whatever you prefer.

If you're up for more of a challenge, try following the directions to create your own Sol LeWitt-inspired picture! After you finish following the directions, color the finished picture. And if you have trouble following the directions, or make a mistake – no worries – you've just created your own personal design!

For those of you who are so inclined, you can also write your own set of instructions. It's an added challenge – and we'd love you to share these instructions on our Facebook page! But, a note of caution, be sure to try out your instructions first to be sure you've included everything necessary. I usually prefer to draw my designs on graph paper. It provides a basic structure to get started. But don't be constrained if you want more freedom. Ignore the boxes or use plain paper. Have fun!

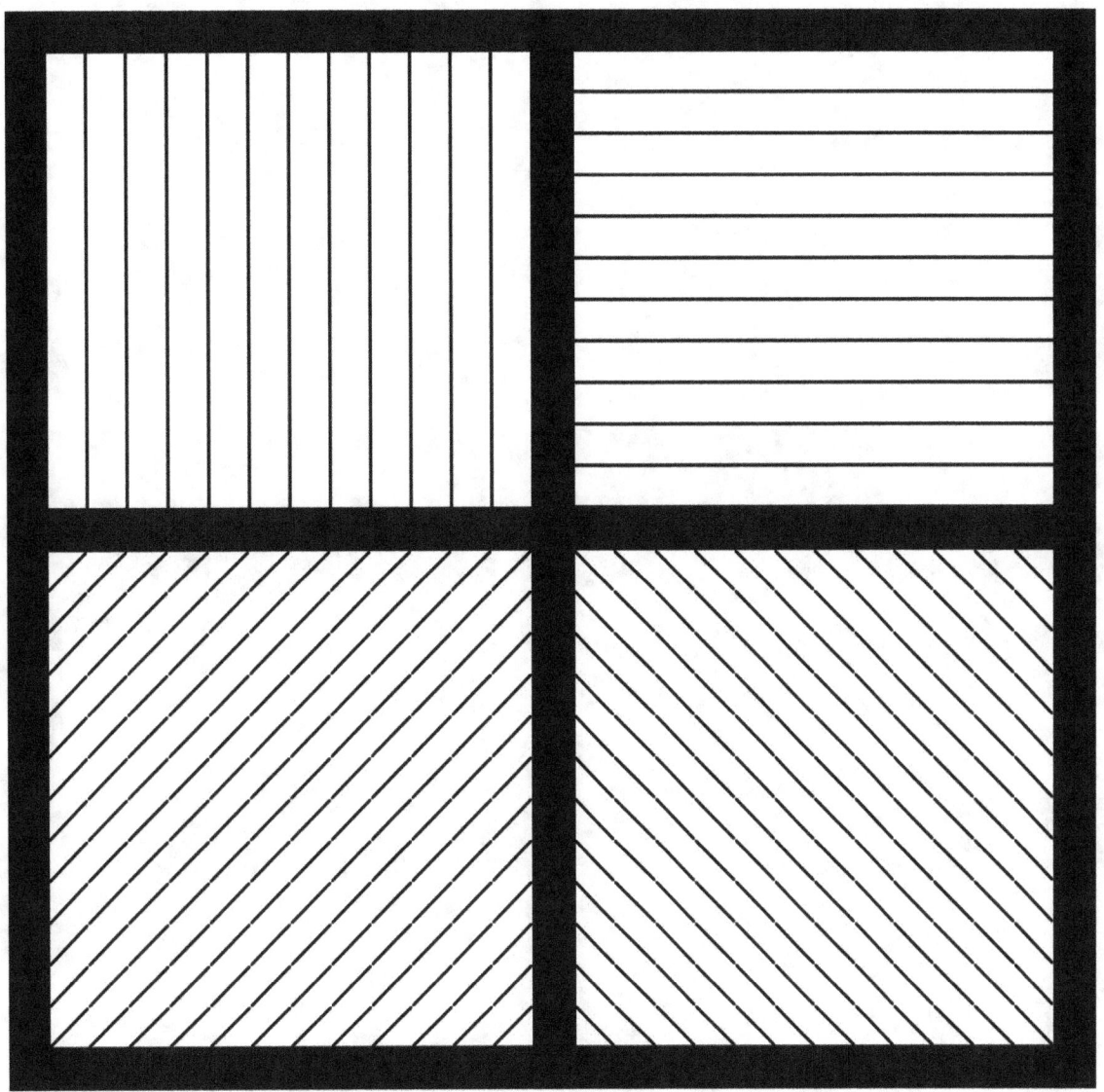

Four squares: Straight lines in four directions.

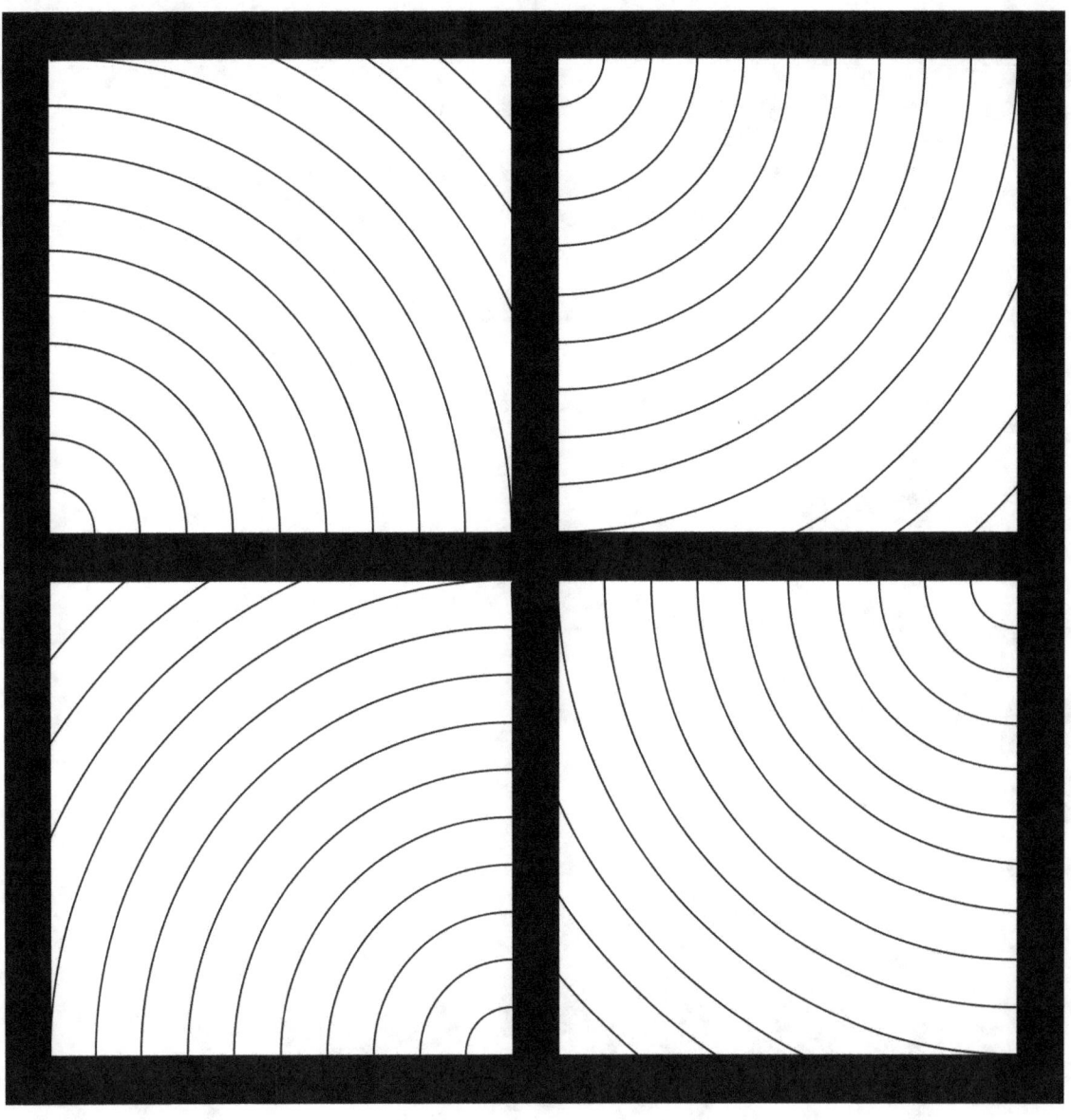

Four squares: Arcs from four corners.

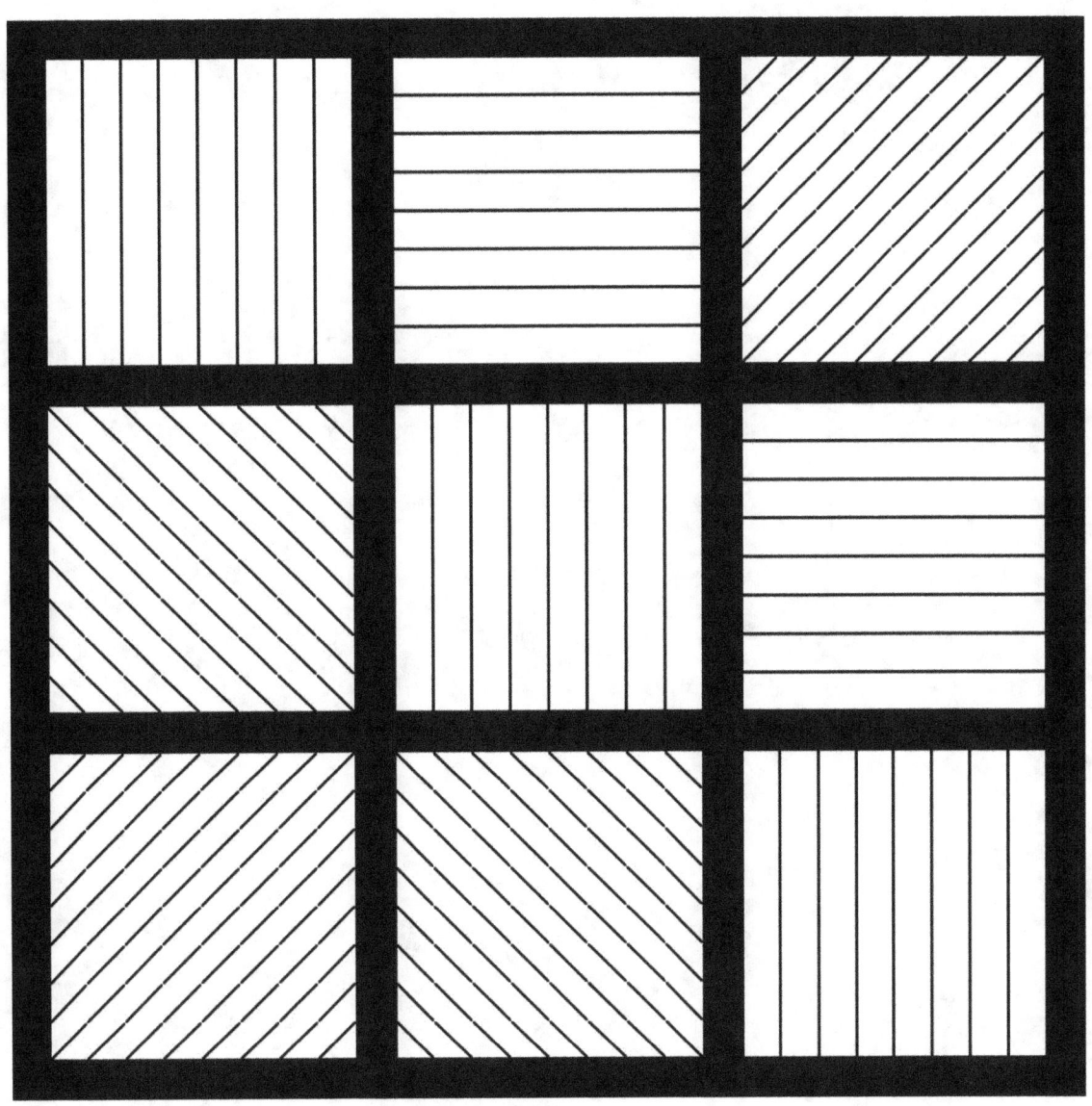

Nine squares: Straight lines in four directions.

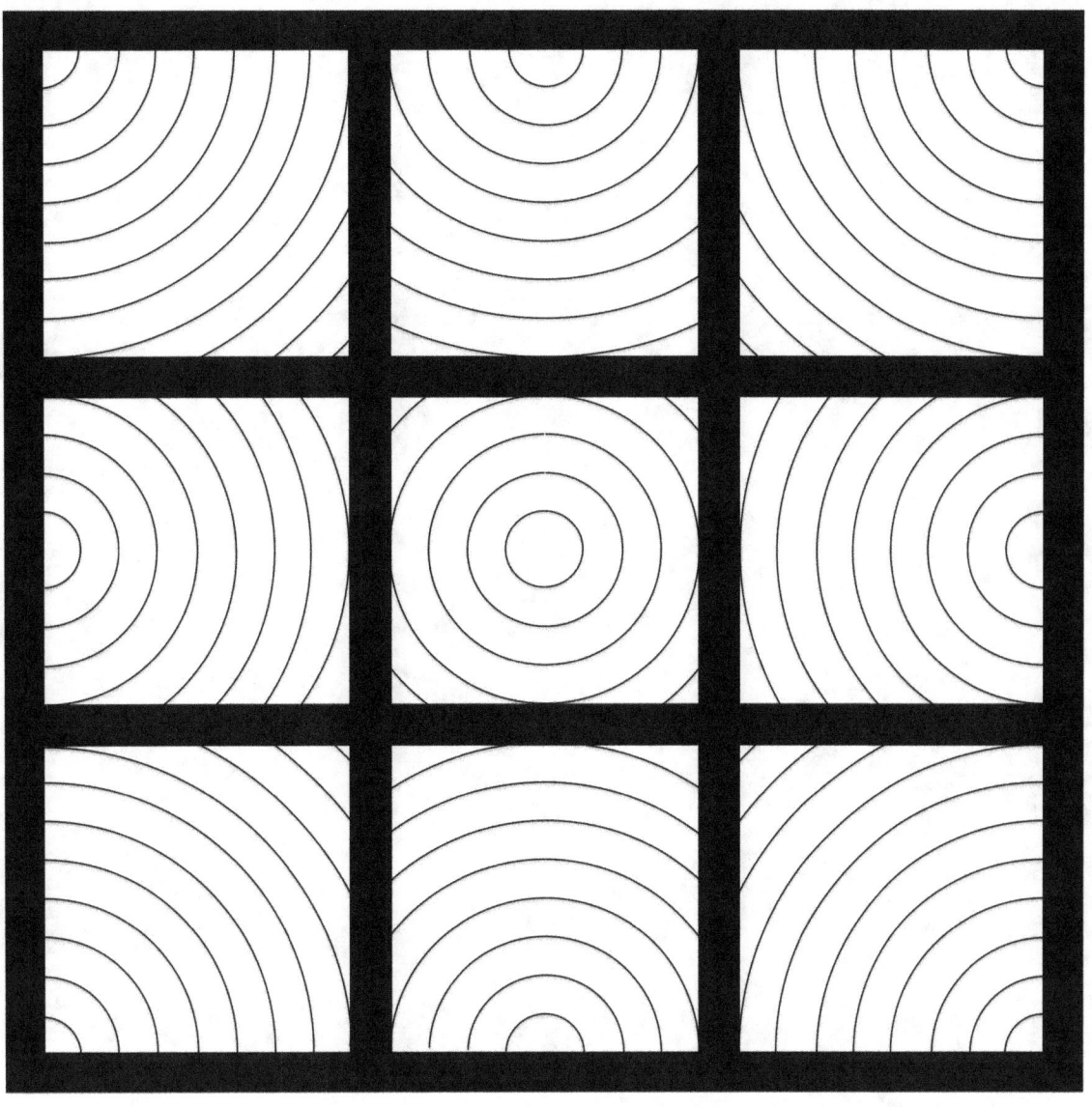

Nine squares: Arcs from four corners, arcs from four sides and arcs from the center.

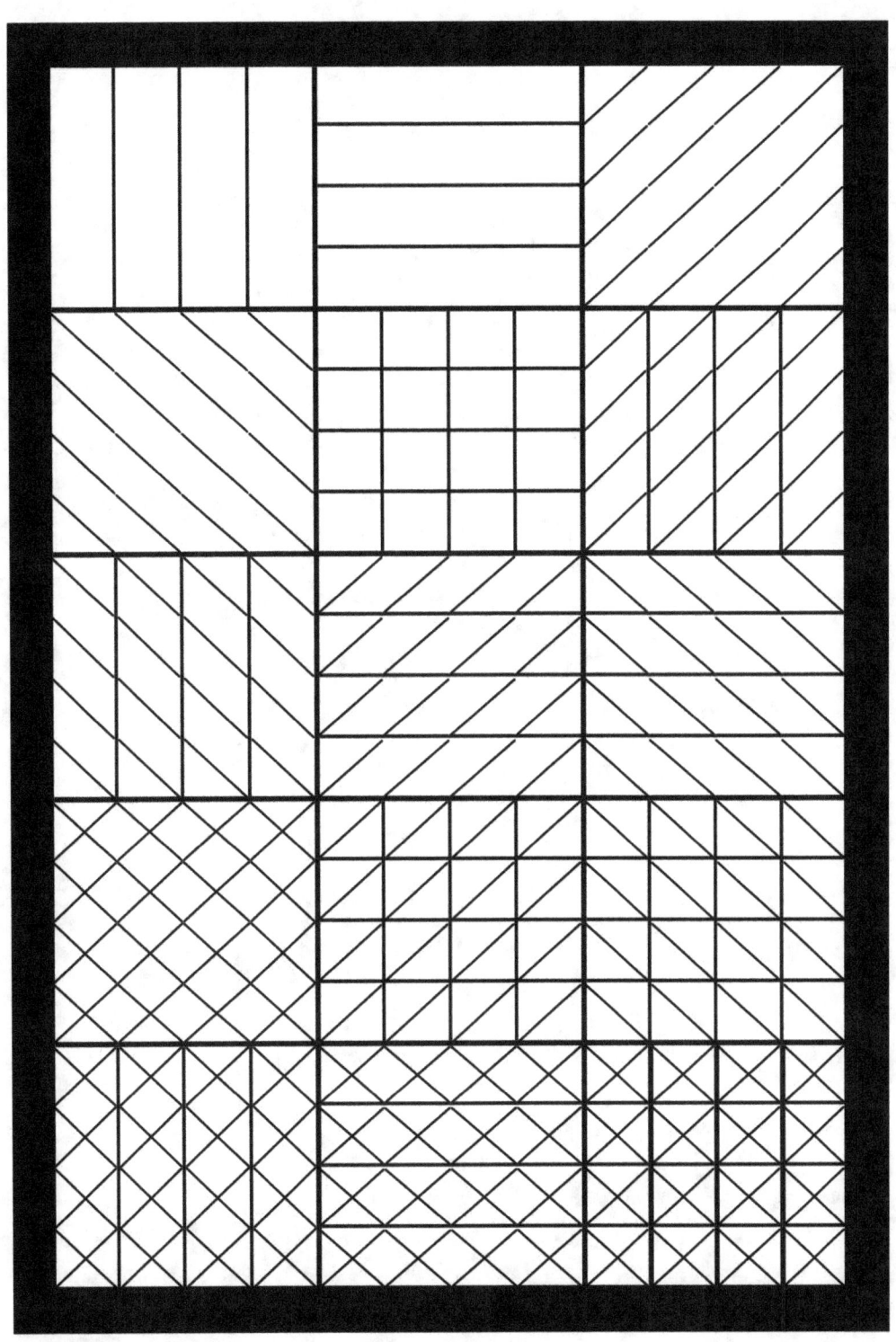

Fifteen squares: all one-, two-, three-, and four-part
combinations of lines in four directions.

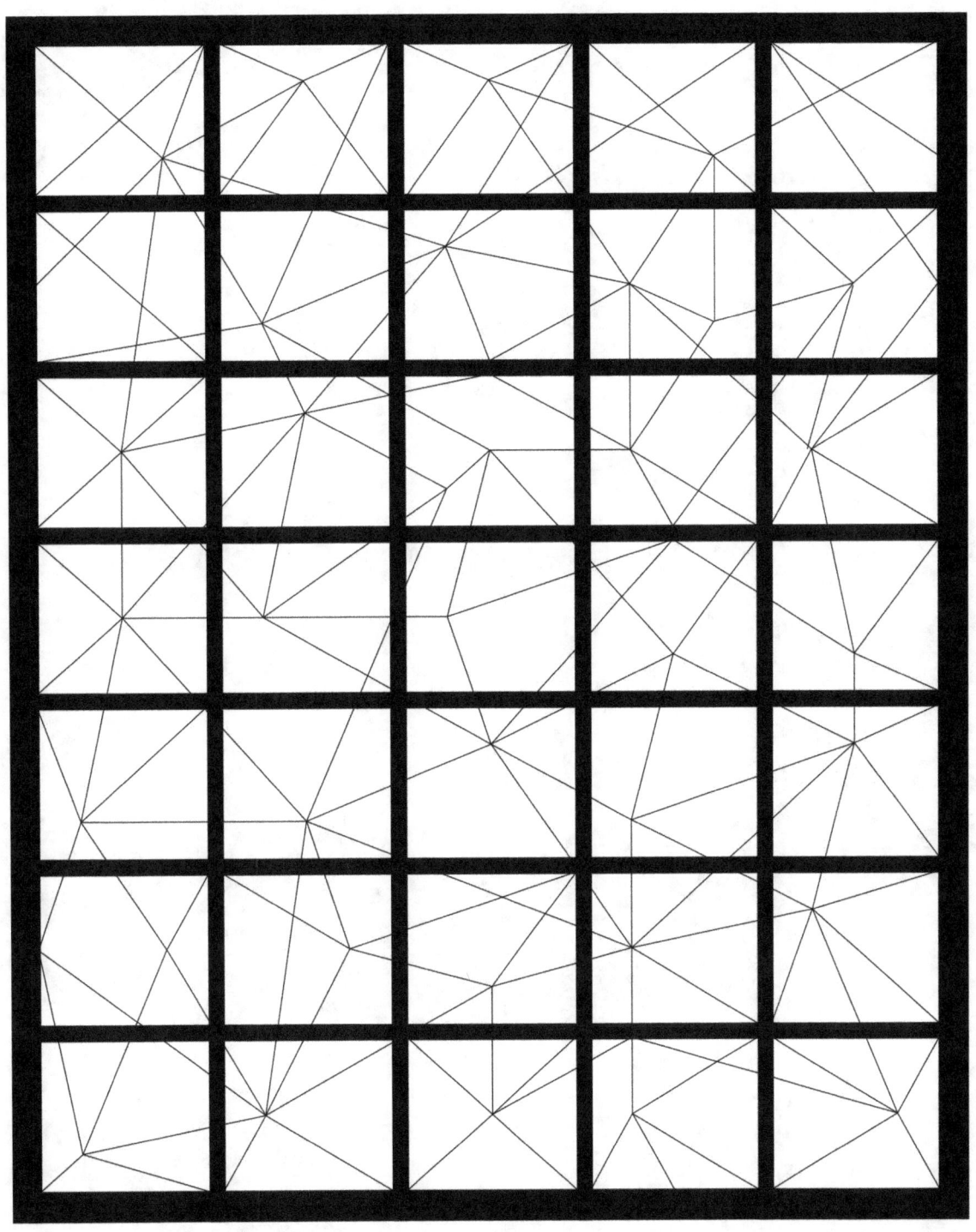

Thirty-five squares: Straight lines connecting points, corners and midpoints.

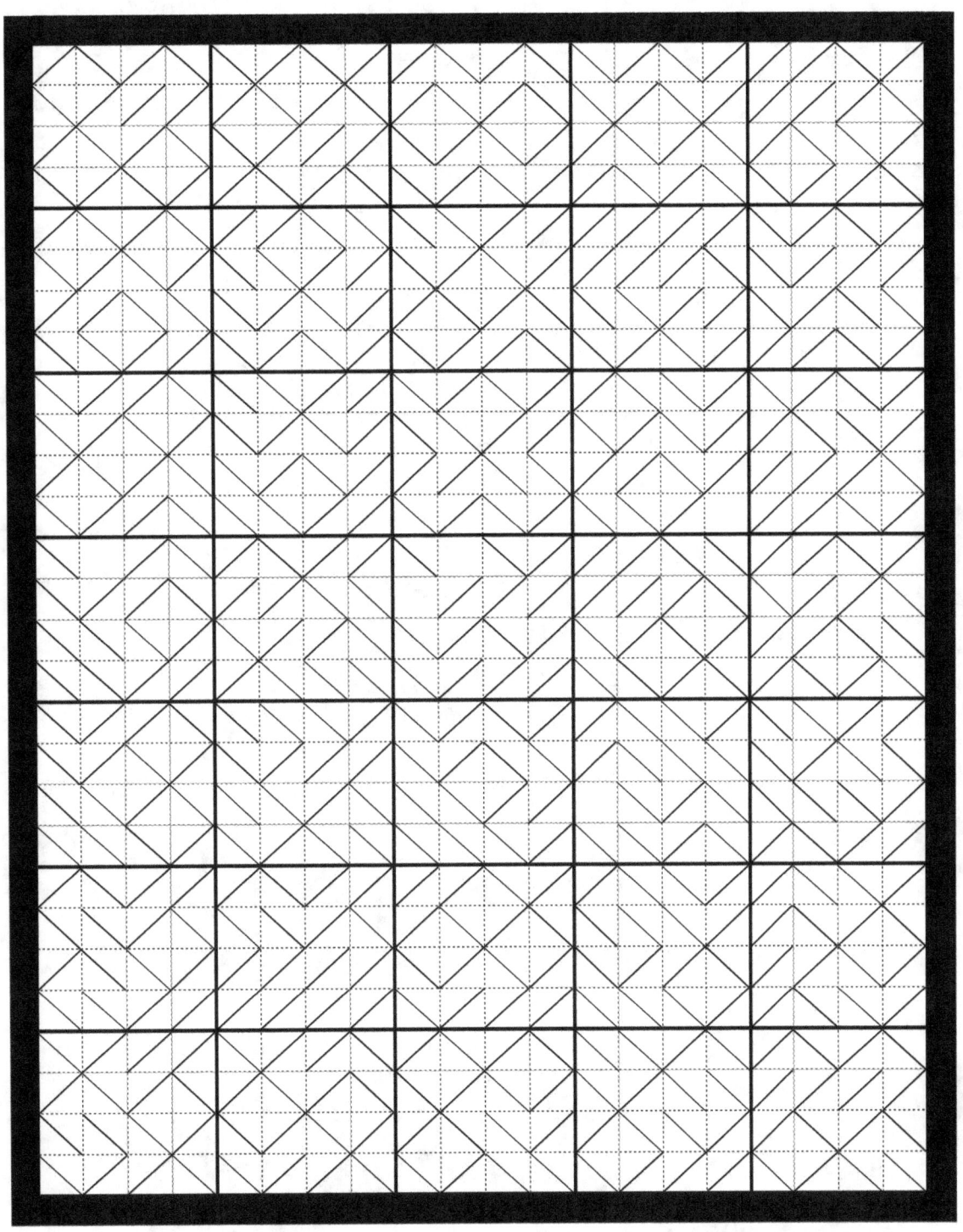

Thirty-five squares: short diagonal lines in all directions,
some touching some not.

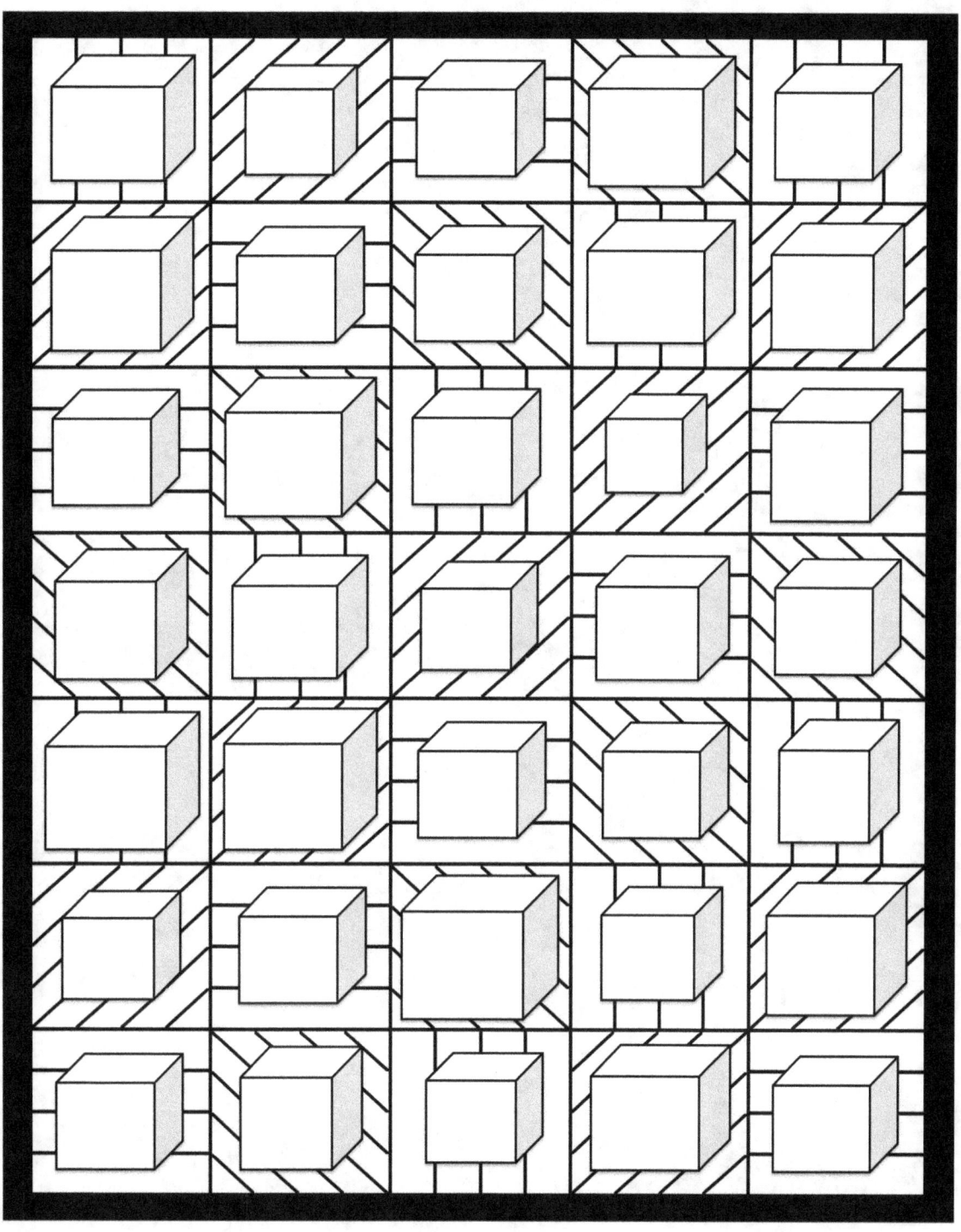

Thirty-five squares: Straight lines in four directions with superimposed cubes.

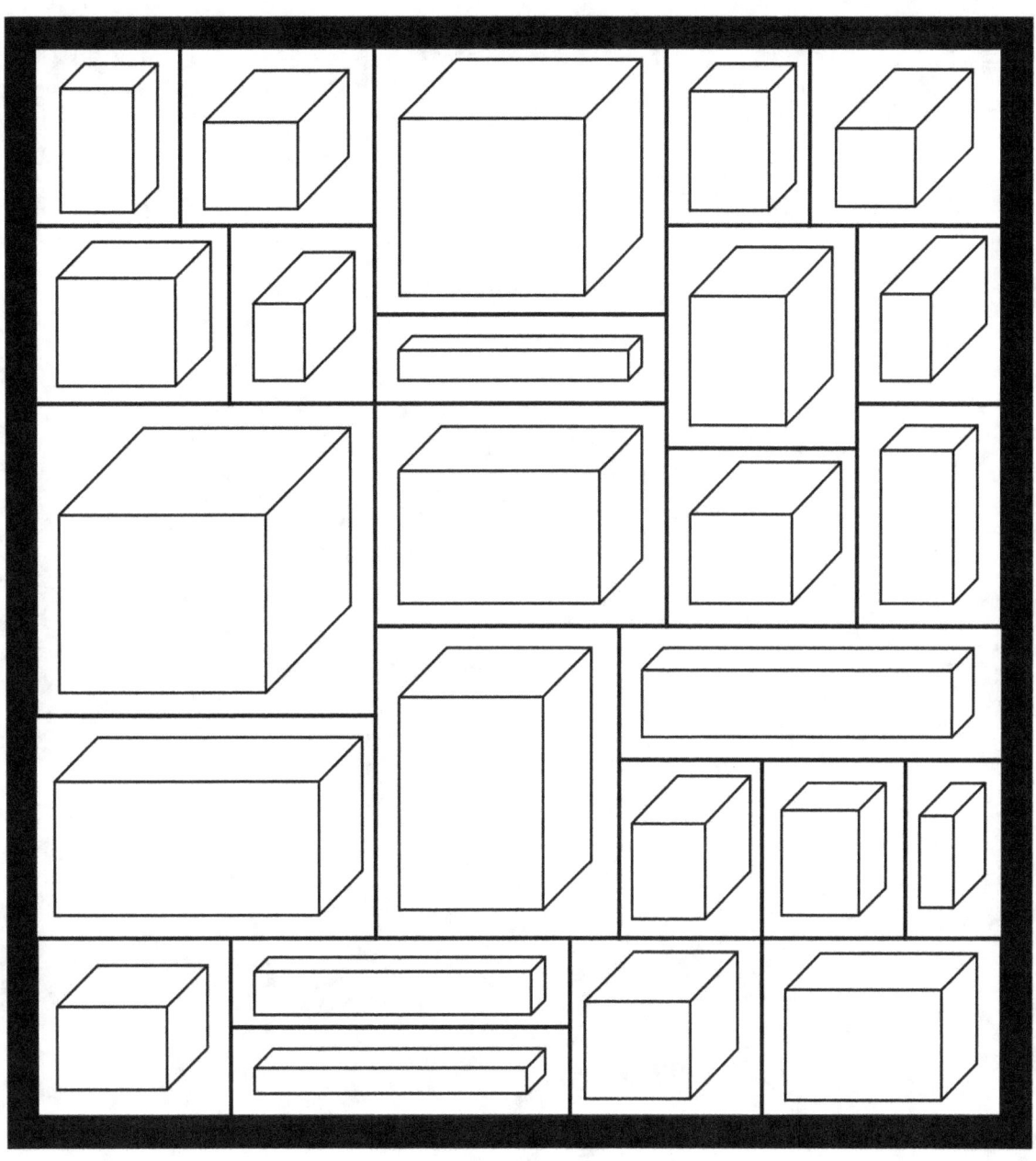

Twenty-one isometric cubes of varying sizes.

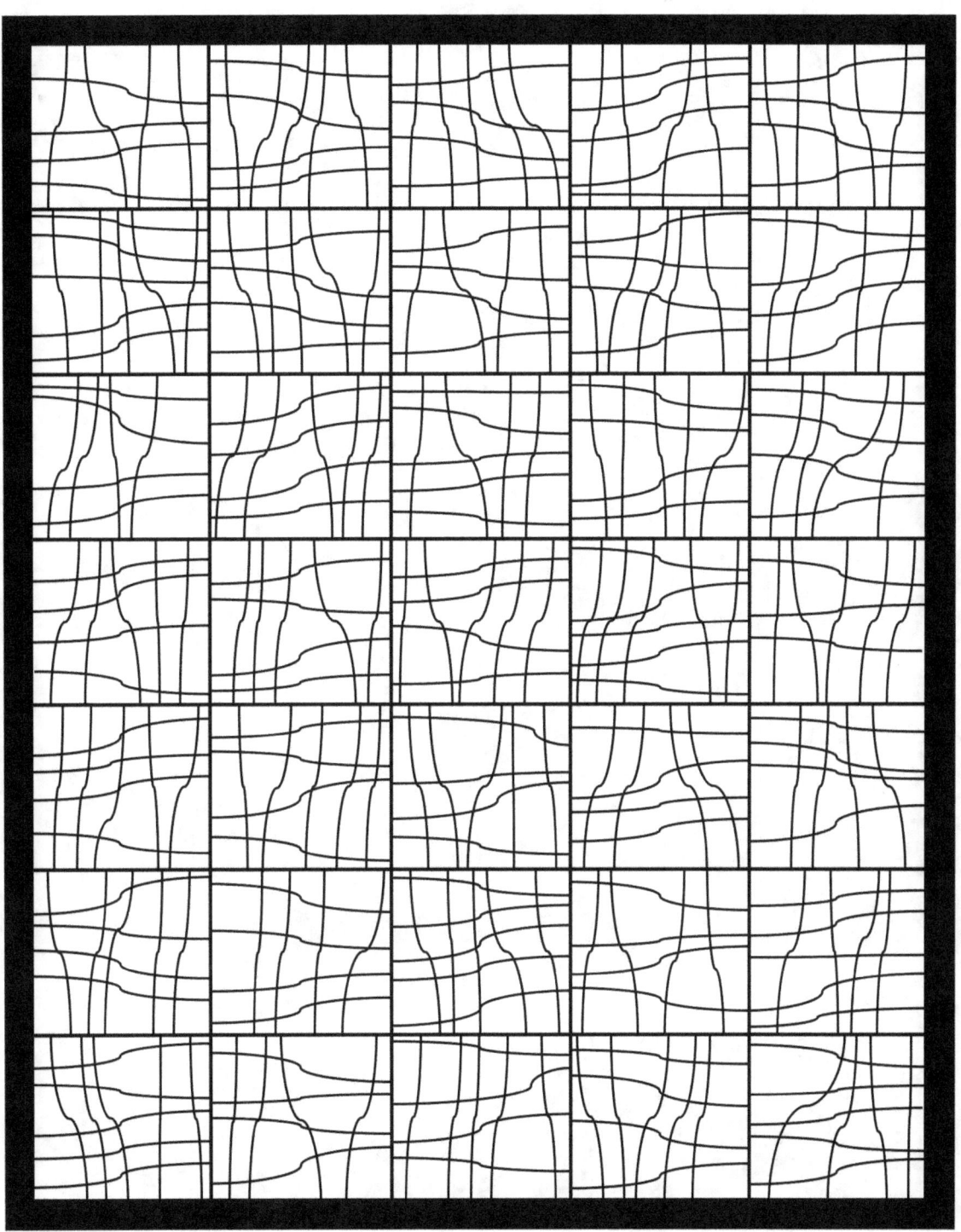

Thirty-five squares: In each square, at least four not-straight lines in two directions.

Geometric Drawings: Follow The Directions

The following directions let you add your own interpretations to provide a little more challenge and allow for more creativity. Some of the directions are straightforward, like the following:

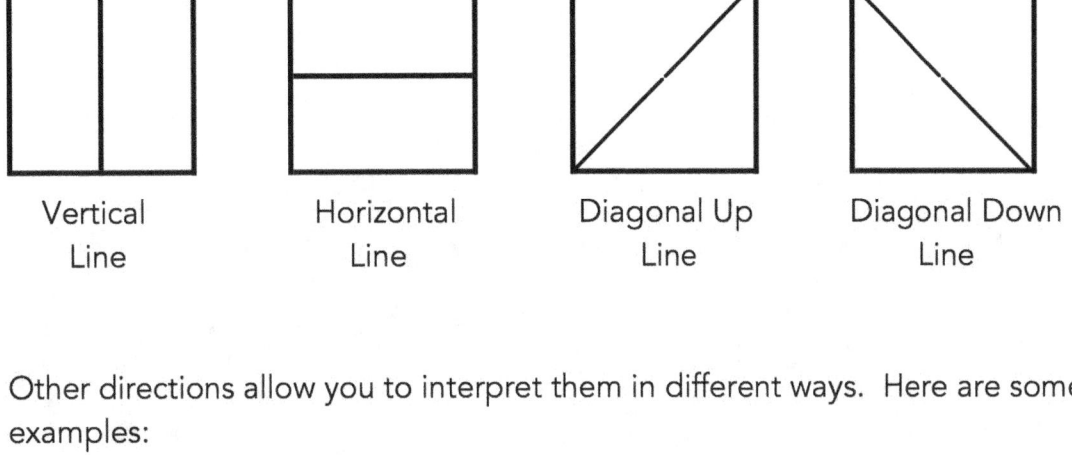

| Vertical Line | Horizontal Line | Diagonal Up Line | Diagonal Down Line |

Other directions allow you to interpret them in different ways. Here are some examples:

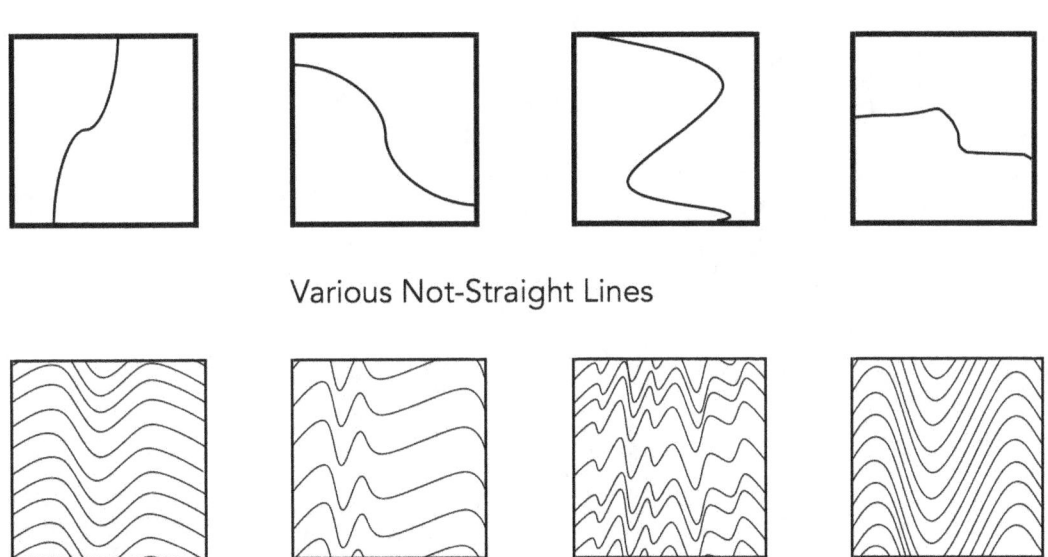

Various Not-Straight Lines

Possible Interpretations of Parallel Horizontal Squiggles

Feel free to add your own flair to these directions and interpret them any way you like. Have fun and enjoy coloring the final product! And please share your work on our facebook page – Sol LeWitt Inspired Coloring Book or via the hashtag #ColorLewitt.

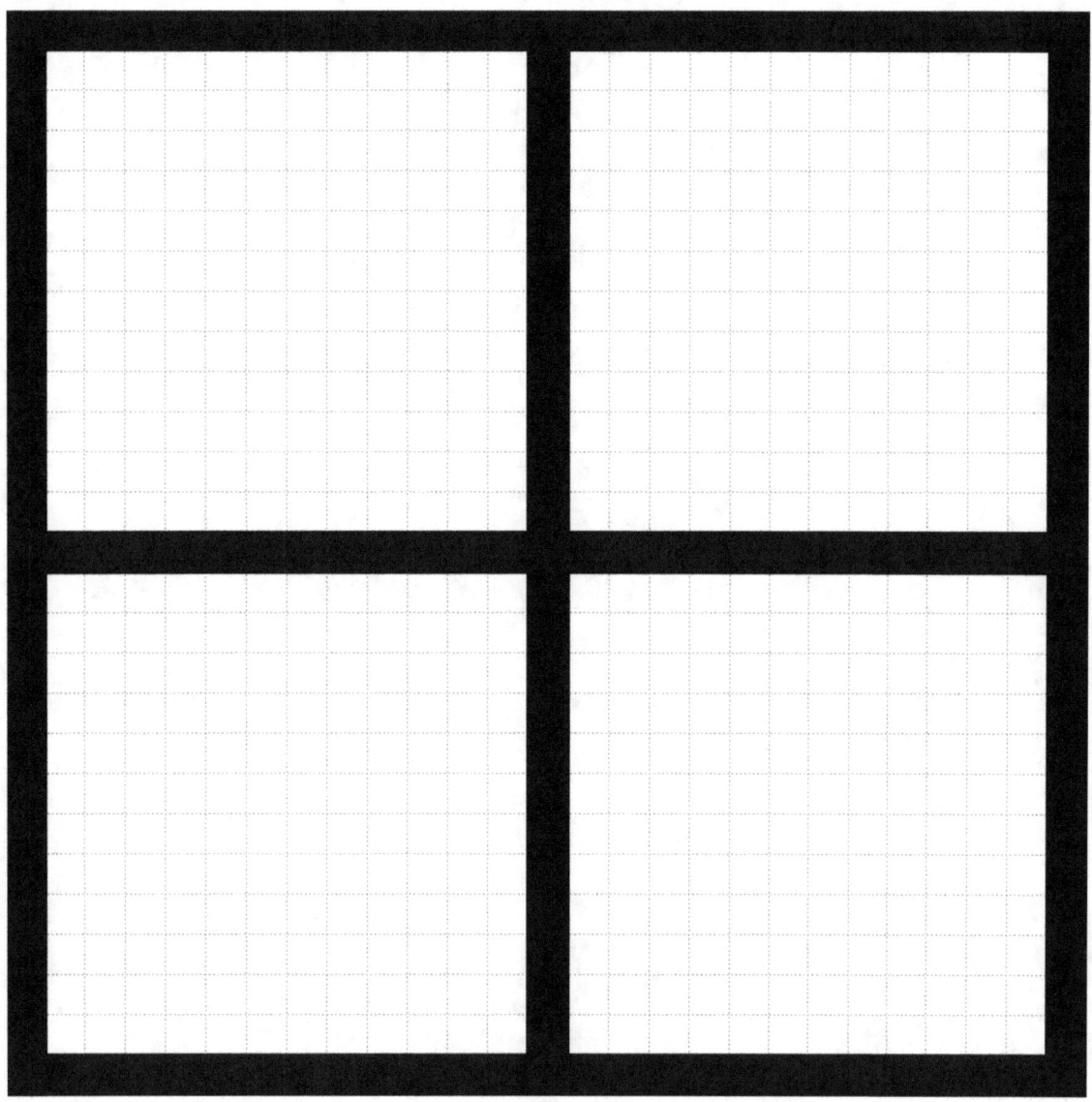

Four squares: Not straight lines in all directions.

In the top left square, make a number of vertical not straight lines. In the top right square, make a number of horizontal not straight lines, In the bottom left square, make a number of diagonal up not straight lines. In the bottom right square, make a number of diagonal down not straight lines. Color.

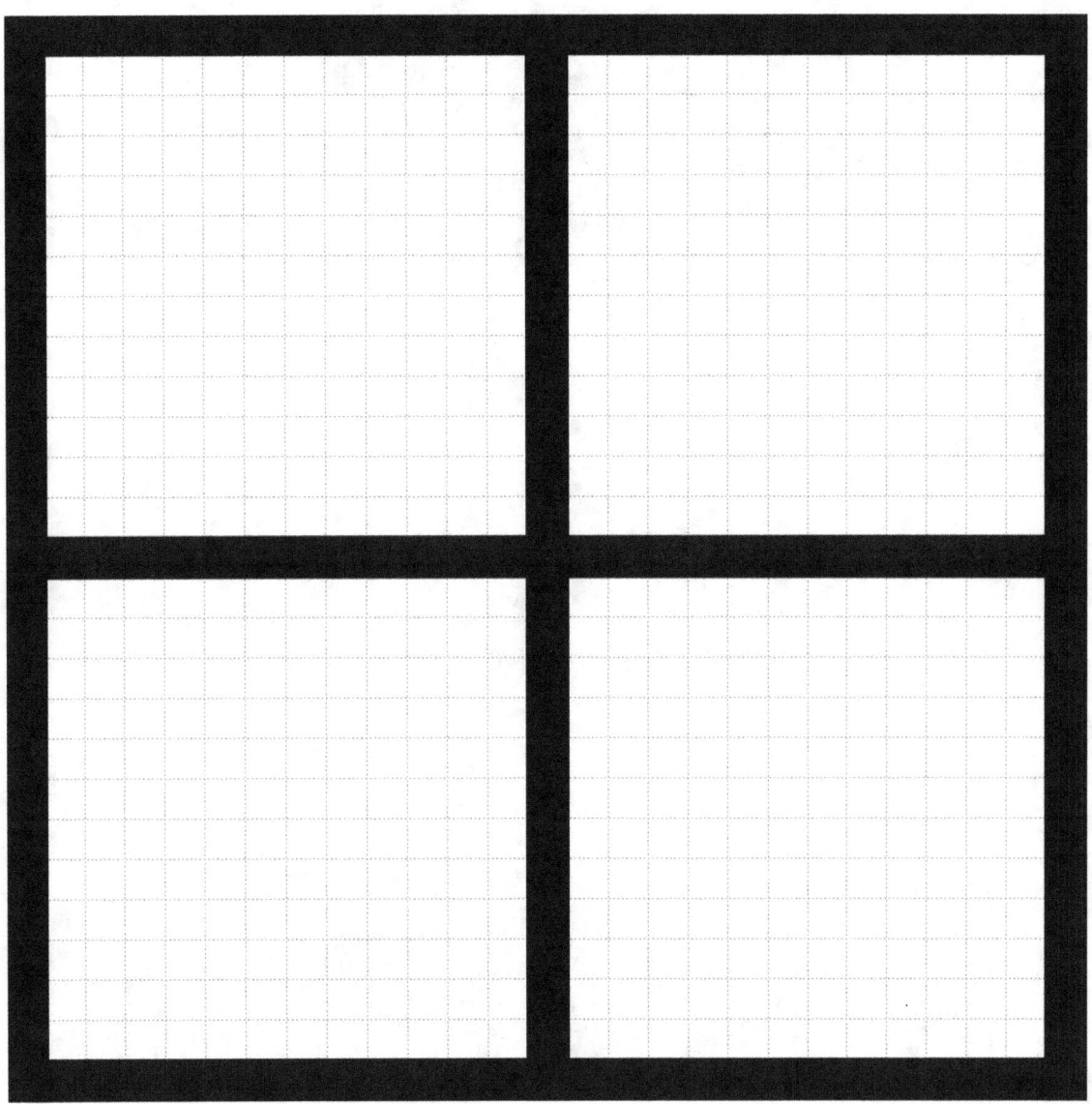

Four squares: Parallel and perpendicular diagonals.

In the first square, draw a diagonal line that slopes downward. In the lower left-side triangle, draw additional diagonal lines parallel to the original diagonal to fill the space with stripes. In the upper right triangle, draw additional lines perpendicular to the original diagonal to fill the space with stripes. Continue in each square with diagonals going in different directions. Color.

An irregular horizontal line repeated in four colors.

Draw a not-straight horizontal line near the top of the paper in black marker. Try to copy it (without touching it) using a red marker. Try copying it again using a yellow marker. Then do the same using a blue marker. Continue repeating this patterns until the bottom of the rectangle is reached.

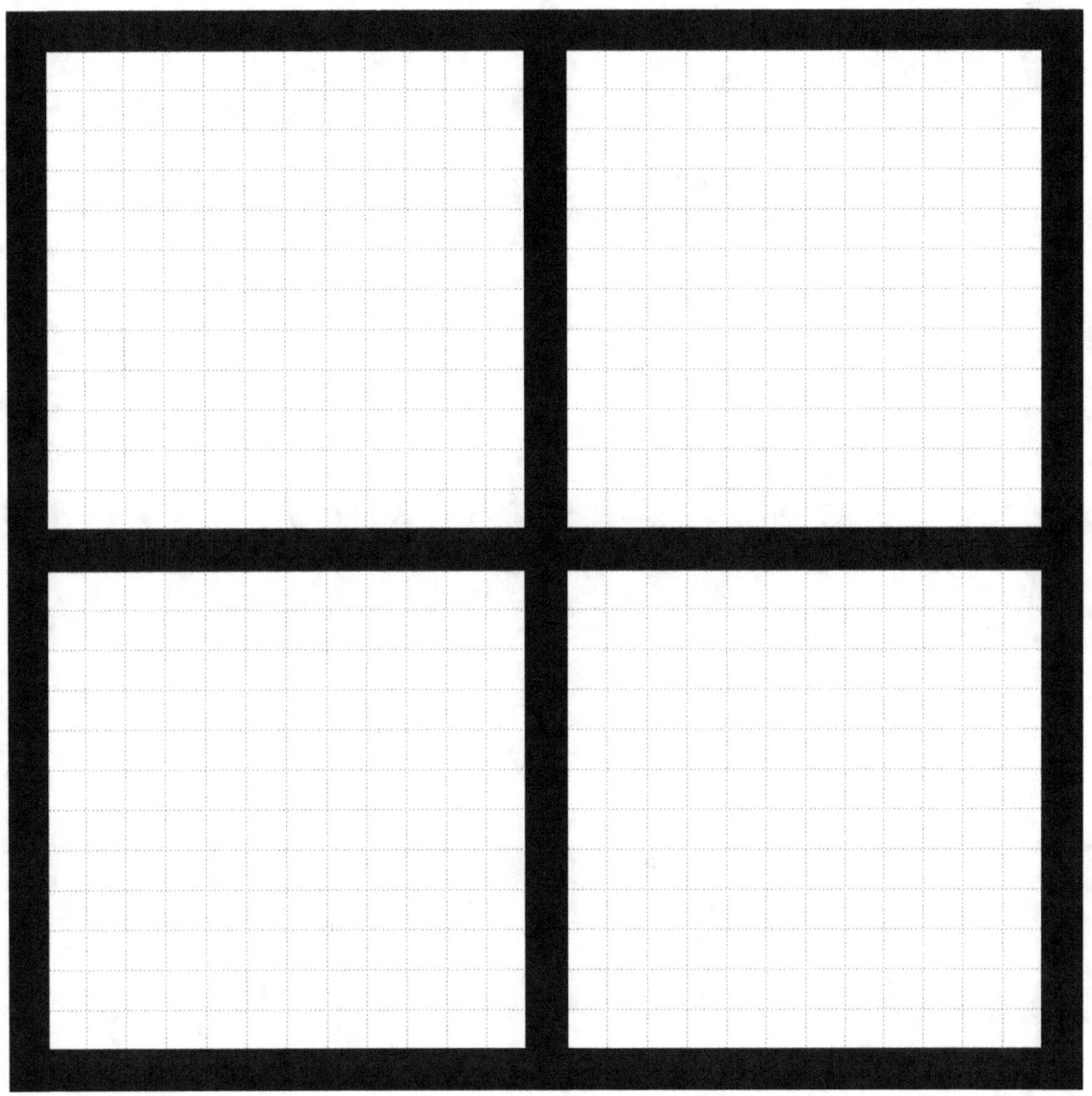

Four squares: Lines radiating from corners.

Draw a number of straight lines that radiate from two different corners of the square. Repeat in each square using a different combination of corners. Color.

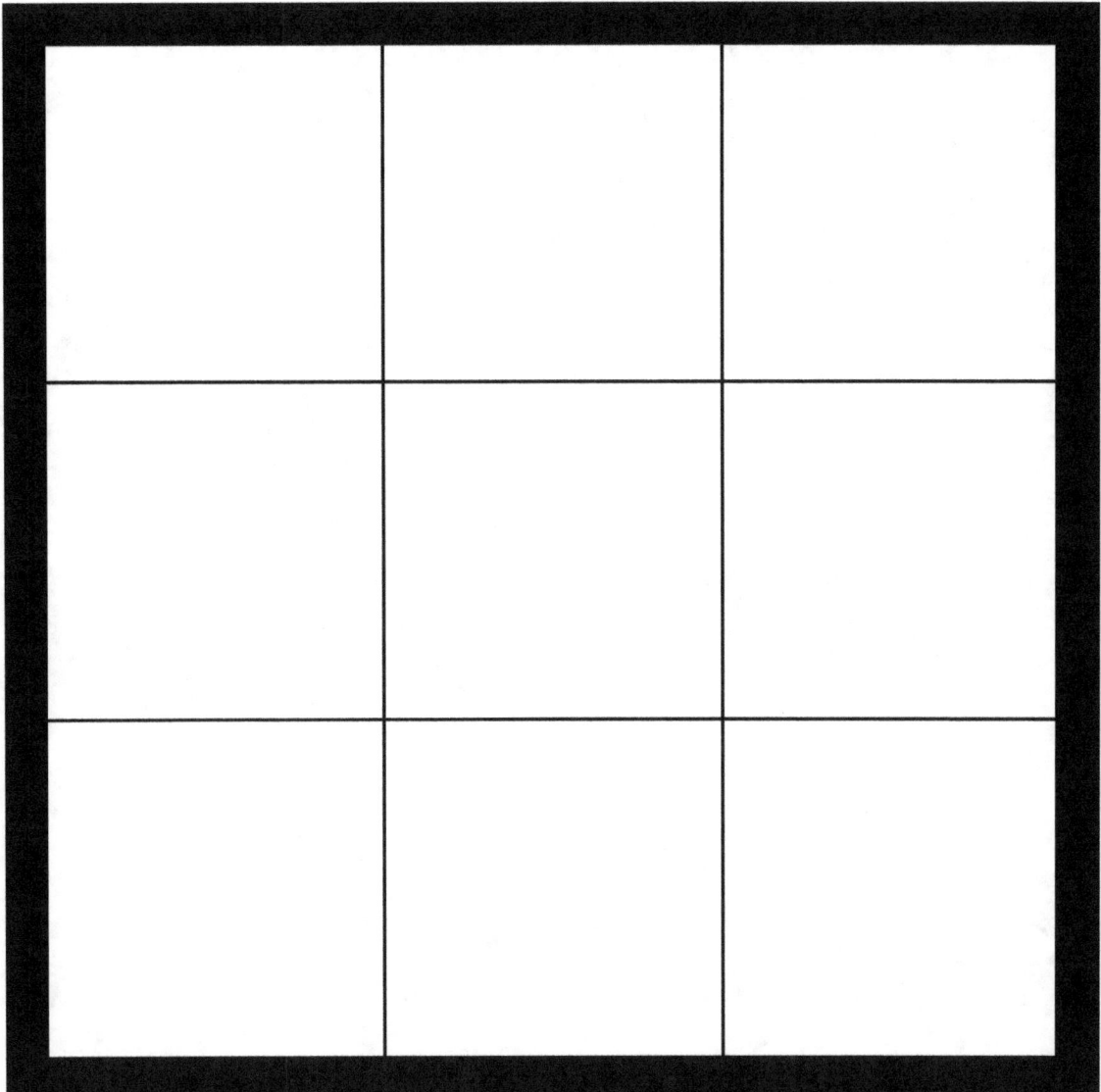

Nine squares: Straight lines connecting points, corners and midpoints.

In each square draw one or two points. Draw lines to connect each point to the corners and midpoints of the square using a straight line. Draw lines to connect the points to other points. Color.

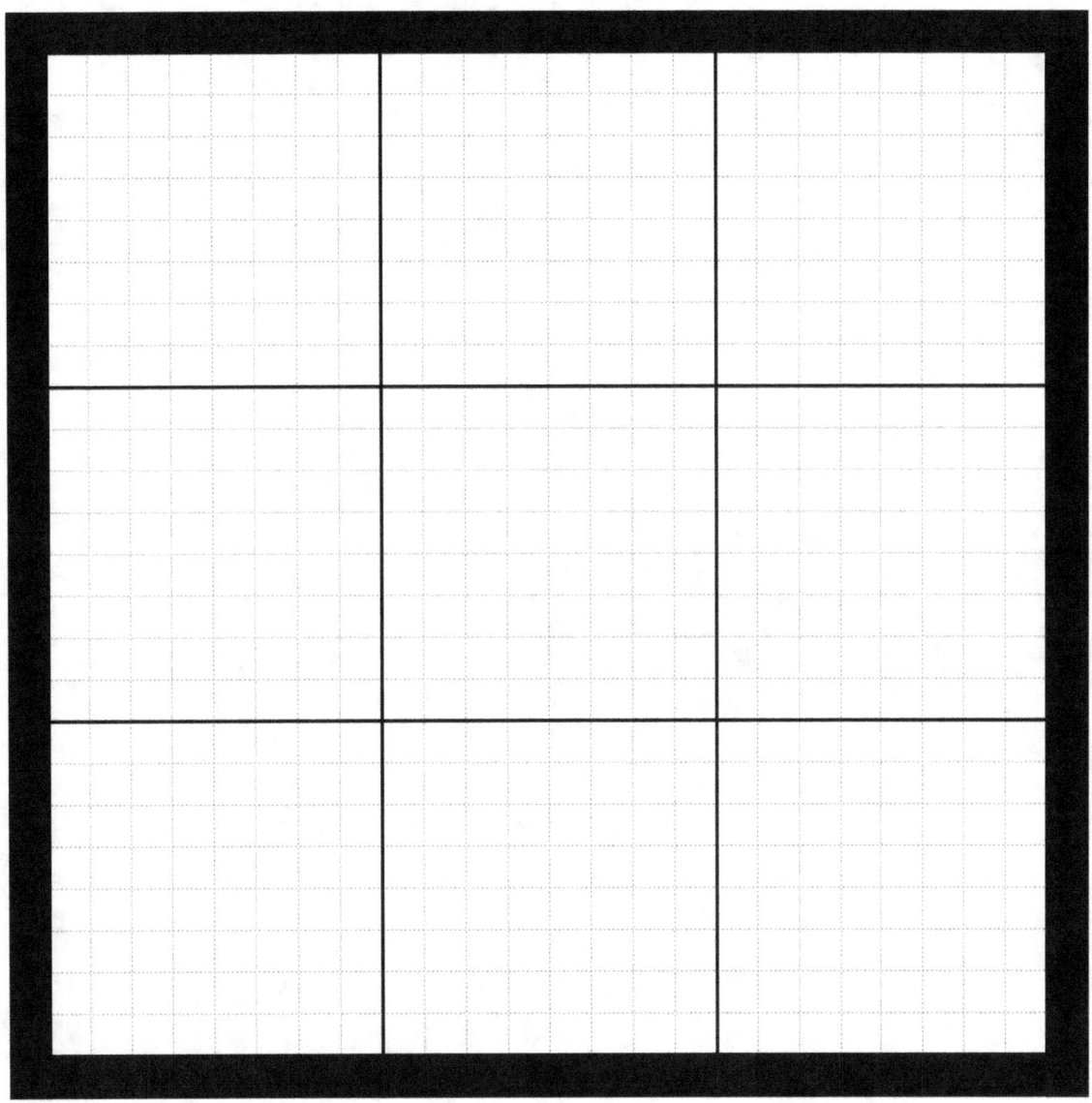

Nine squares: Parallel lines and squiggles.

Fill every other square with parallel horizontal squiggles. Fill the remaining squares with parallel straight lines – in all directions. Color.

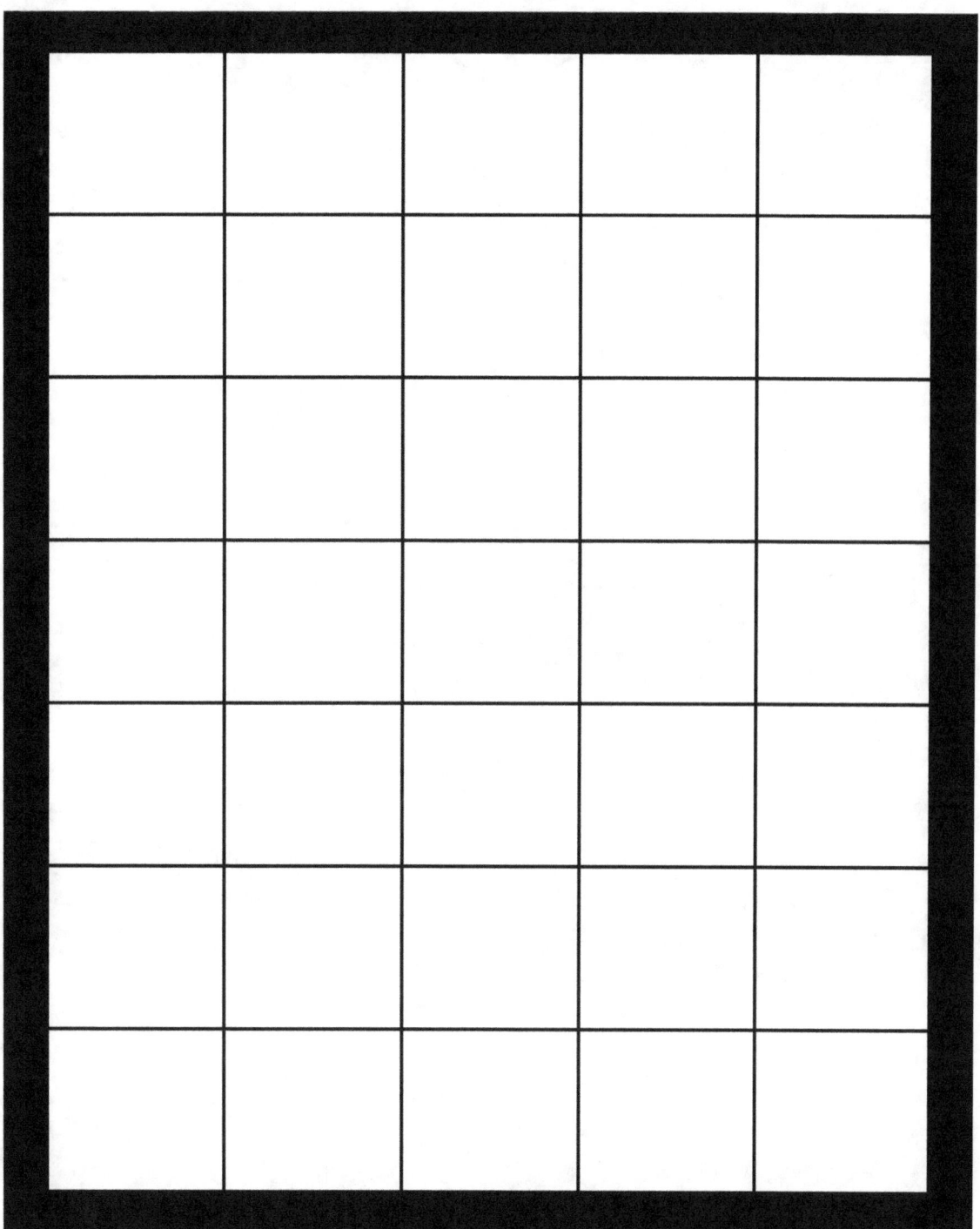

Thirty-five squares: Not straight lines in two directions.

In each square, draw at least four vertical not-straight lines and at least 4 horizontal not-straight lines. Color.

Combination Drawings

The following pictures are based on LeWitt's combination drawings, where LeWitt combines simple lines and shapes, two at a time, to create beautiful patterns. These combination drawings start with a set number of basic elements – lines, curves, and shapes – and then combine these in all possible combinations of two. The patterns are then placed into a rectangular shape to form a finished picture.

As you can see in the following pages, the first step is to decide the number of elements you want to use. I've provided templates for 6, 8 and 10 element pictures. You can create your own templates for other possibilities. Once the number of elements is set, choose what elements you want to use. Be sure to pick elements that, when combined together, will create a pleasing design – leaving space to color and not just overlapping each other. Then, use the template to begin to methodically combine element 1 with element 2, 3, 4 and so on. Once you've combined the first element with all the rest, move on to element 2 and combine it with 3, 4, and so on.

Once the template is completed, copy your designs in to the rectangle provided. You can add your designs in the same order as on the template – or mix them up. Then, color the resulting design to create your own Sol LeWitt inspired combination drawing!

4 ELEMENTS - COMBINED TWO AT A TIME

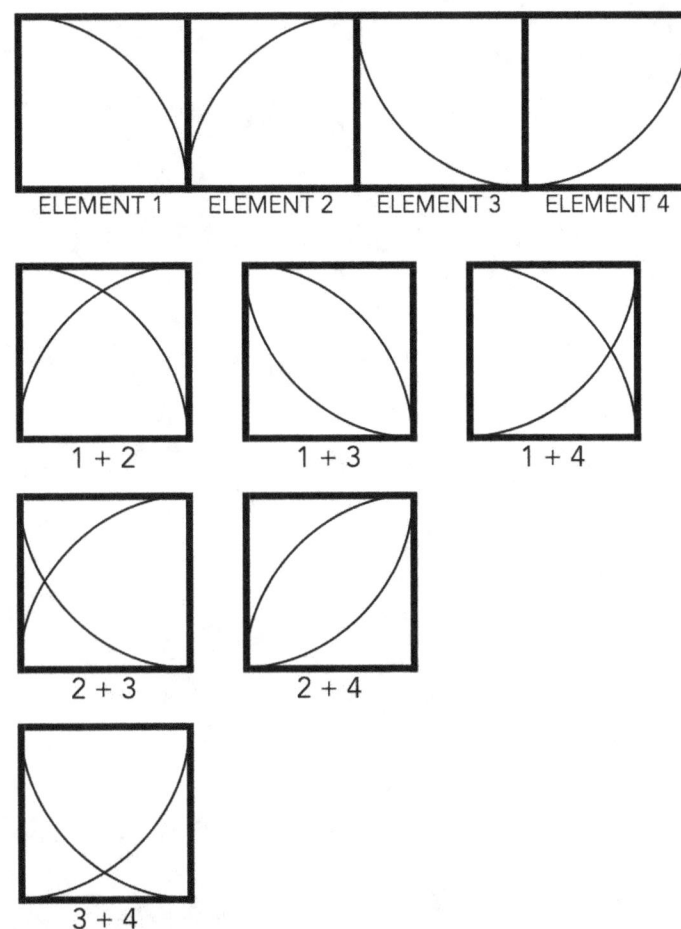

ELEMENT 1   ELEMENT 2   ELEMENT 3   ELEMENT 4

1 + 2   1 + 3   1 + 4

2 + 3   2 + 4

3 + 4

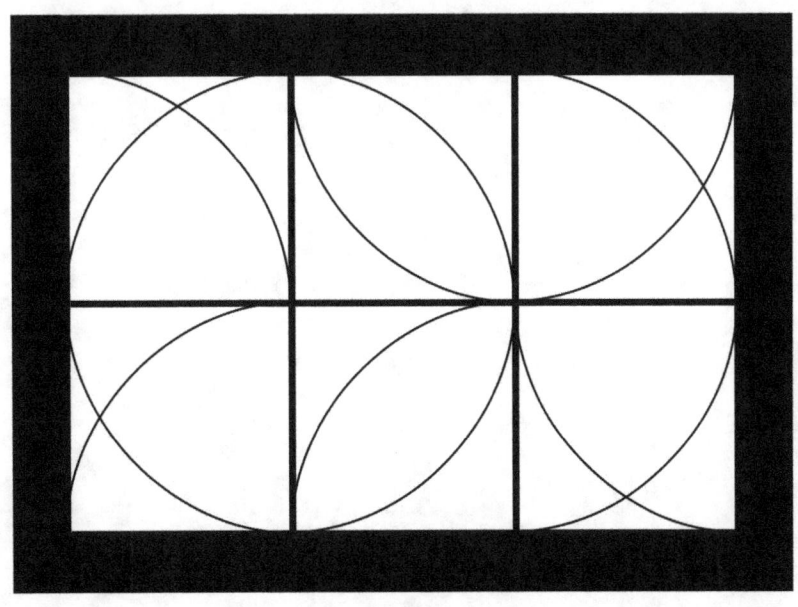

4 ELEMENTS - COMBINED TWO AT A TIME

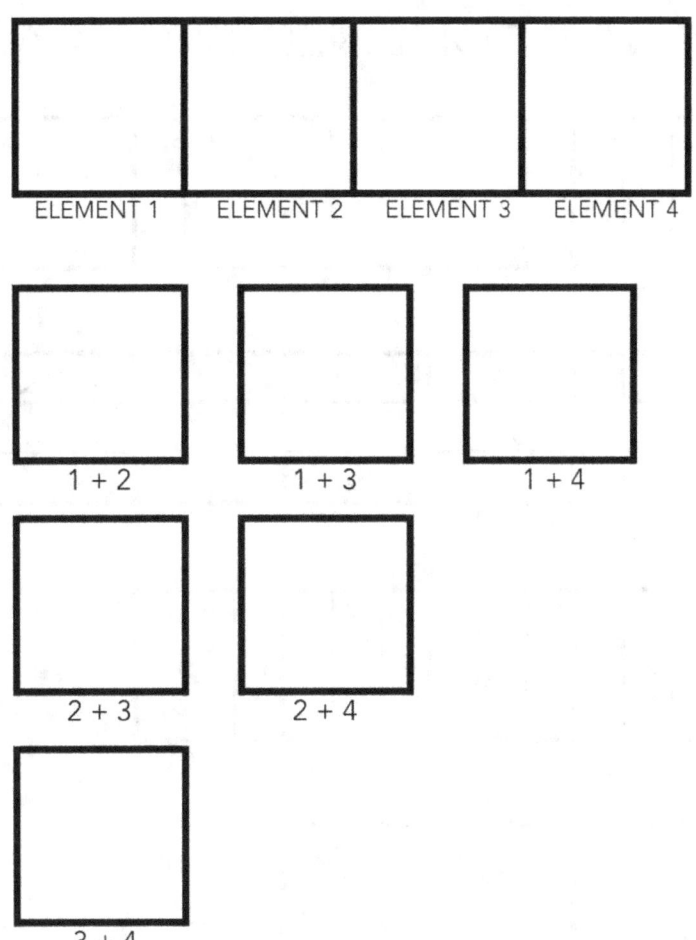

ELEMENT 1   ELEMENT 2   ELEMENT 3   ELEMENT 4

1 + 2   1 + 3   1 + 4

2 + 3   2 + 4

3 + 4

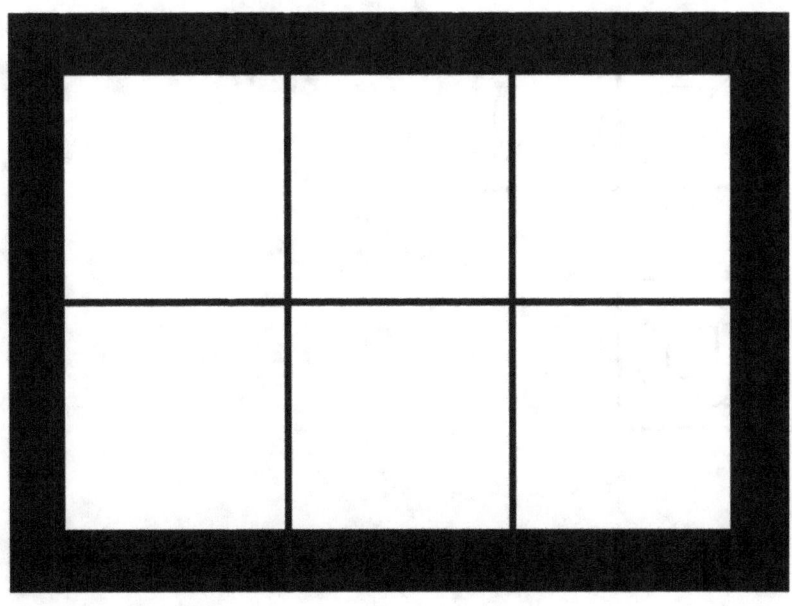

6 ELEMENTS - COMBINED TWO AT A TIME

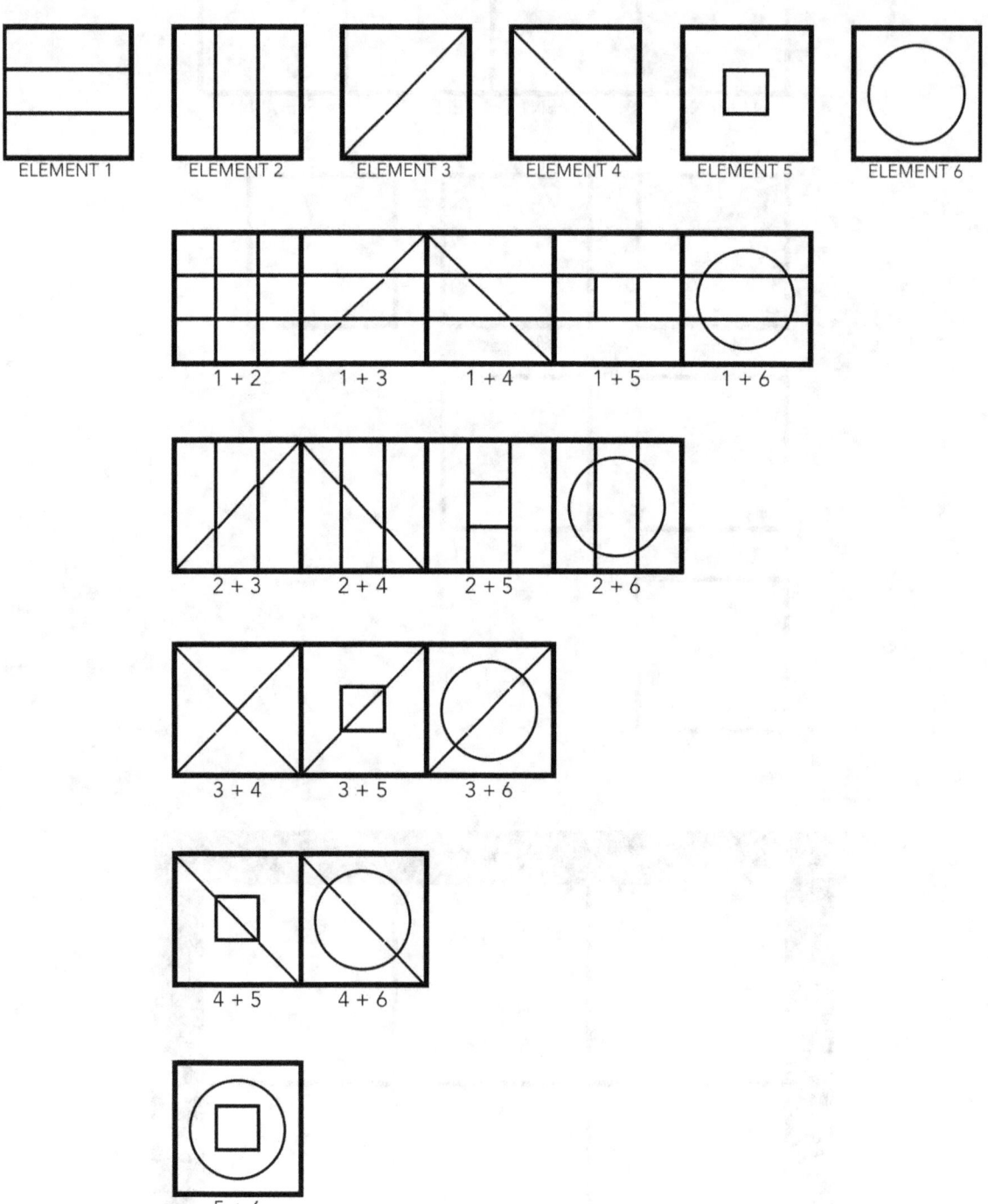

ELEMENT 1 ELEMENT 2 ELEMENT 3 ELEMENT 4 ELEMENT 5 ELEMENT 6

1 + 2   1 + 3   1 + 4   1 + 5   1 + 6

2 + 3   2 + 4   2 + 5   2 + 6

3 + 4   3 + 5   3 + 6

4 + 5   4 + 6

5 + 6

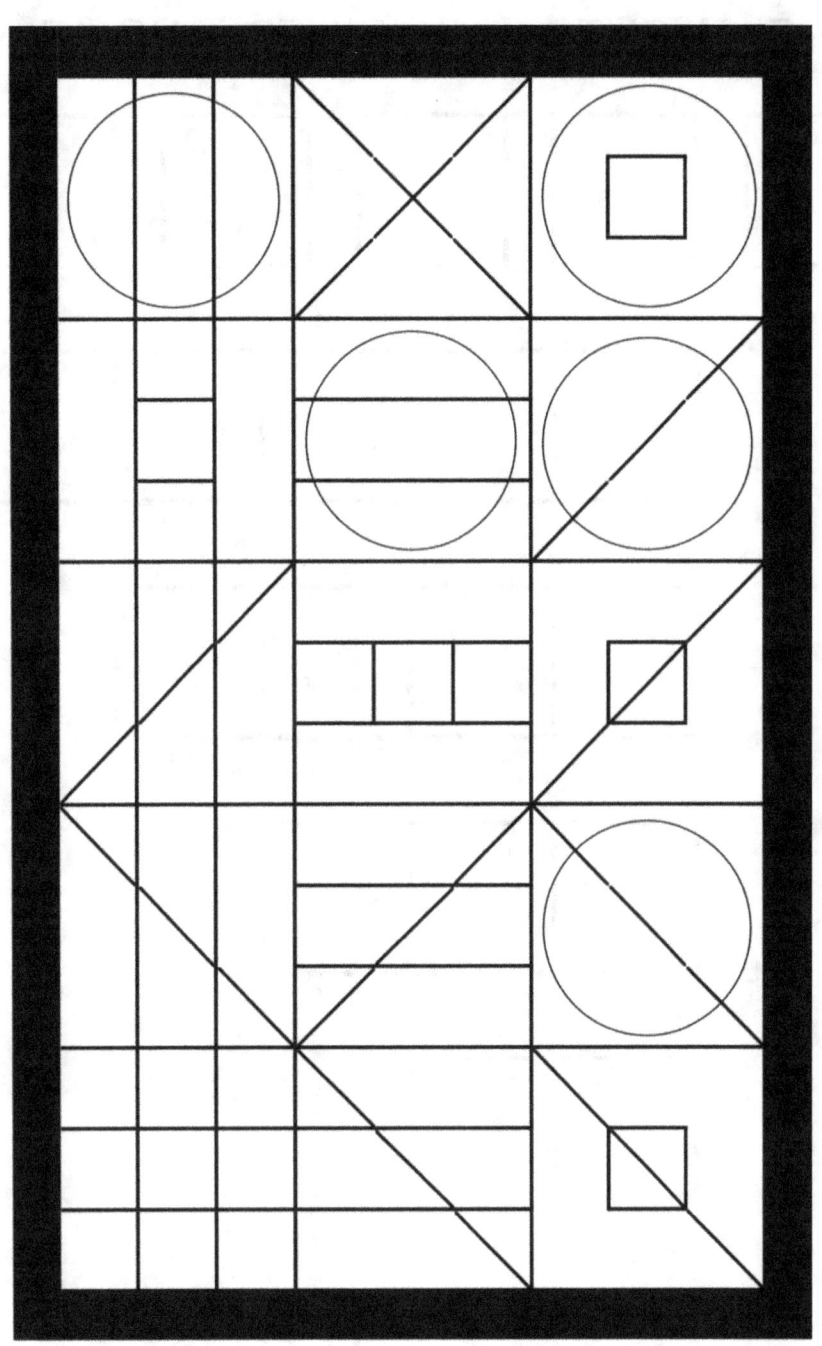

49

6 ELEMENTS - COMBINED TWO AT A TIME

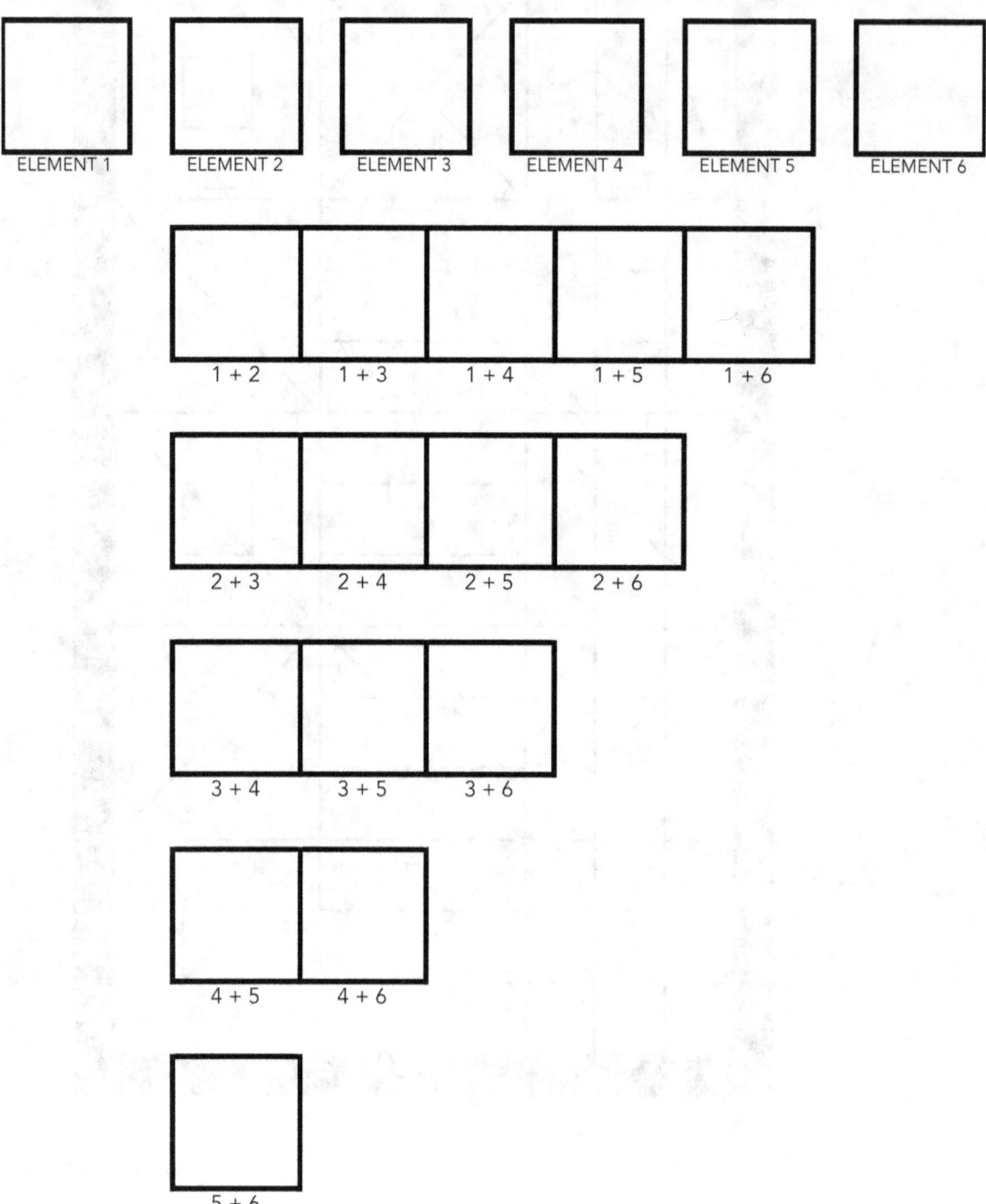

ELEMENT 1　ELEMENT 2　ELEMENT 3　ELEMENT 4　ELEMENT 5　ELEMENT 6

1 + 2　　1 + 3　　1 + 4　　1 + 5　　1 + 6

2 + 3　　2 + 4　　2 + 5　　2 + 6

3 + 4　　3 + 5　　3 + 6

4 + 5　　4 + 6

5 + 6

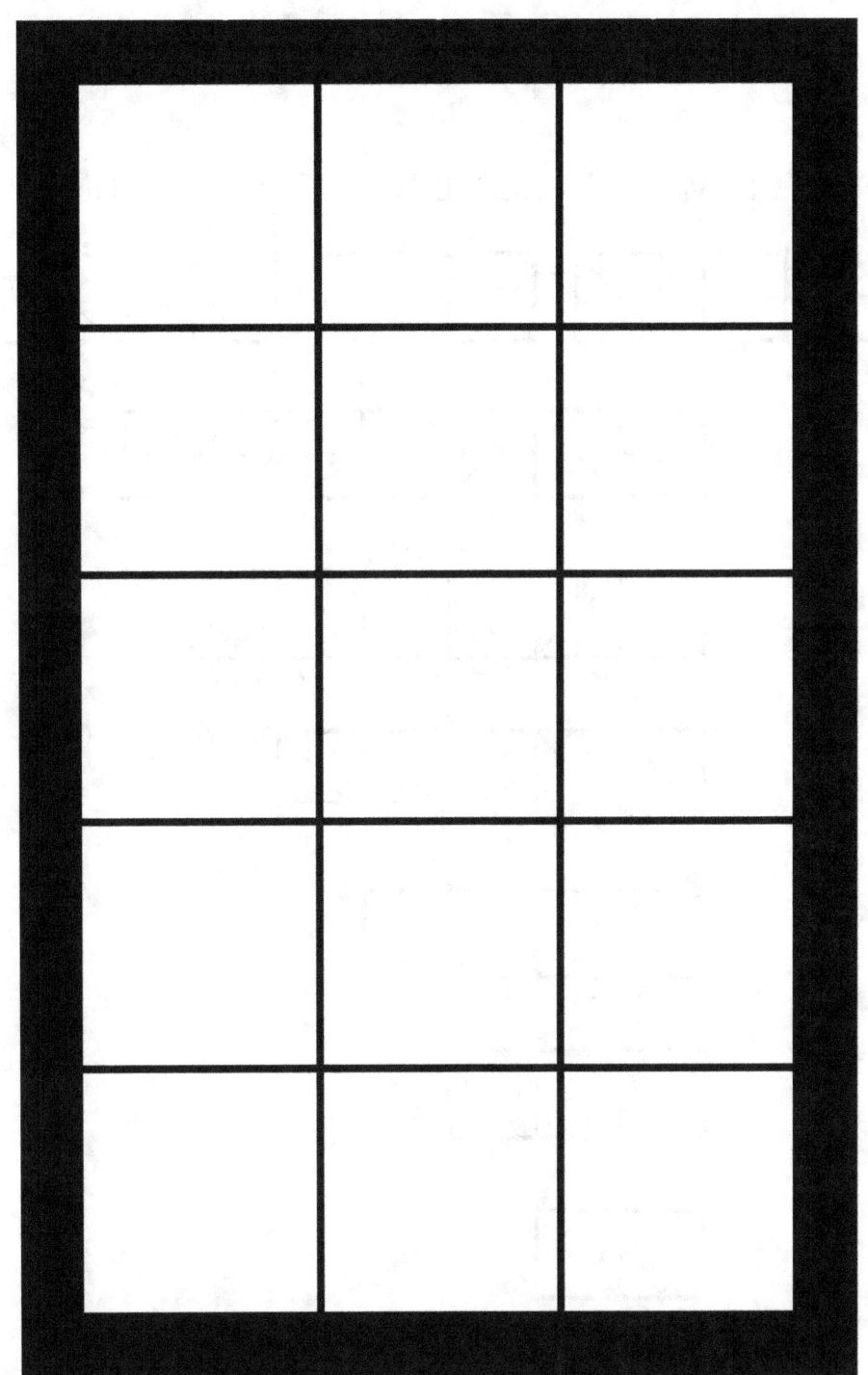

8 ELEMENTS - COMBINED TWO AT A TIME

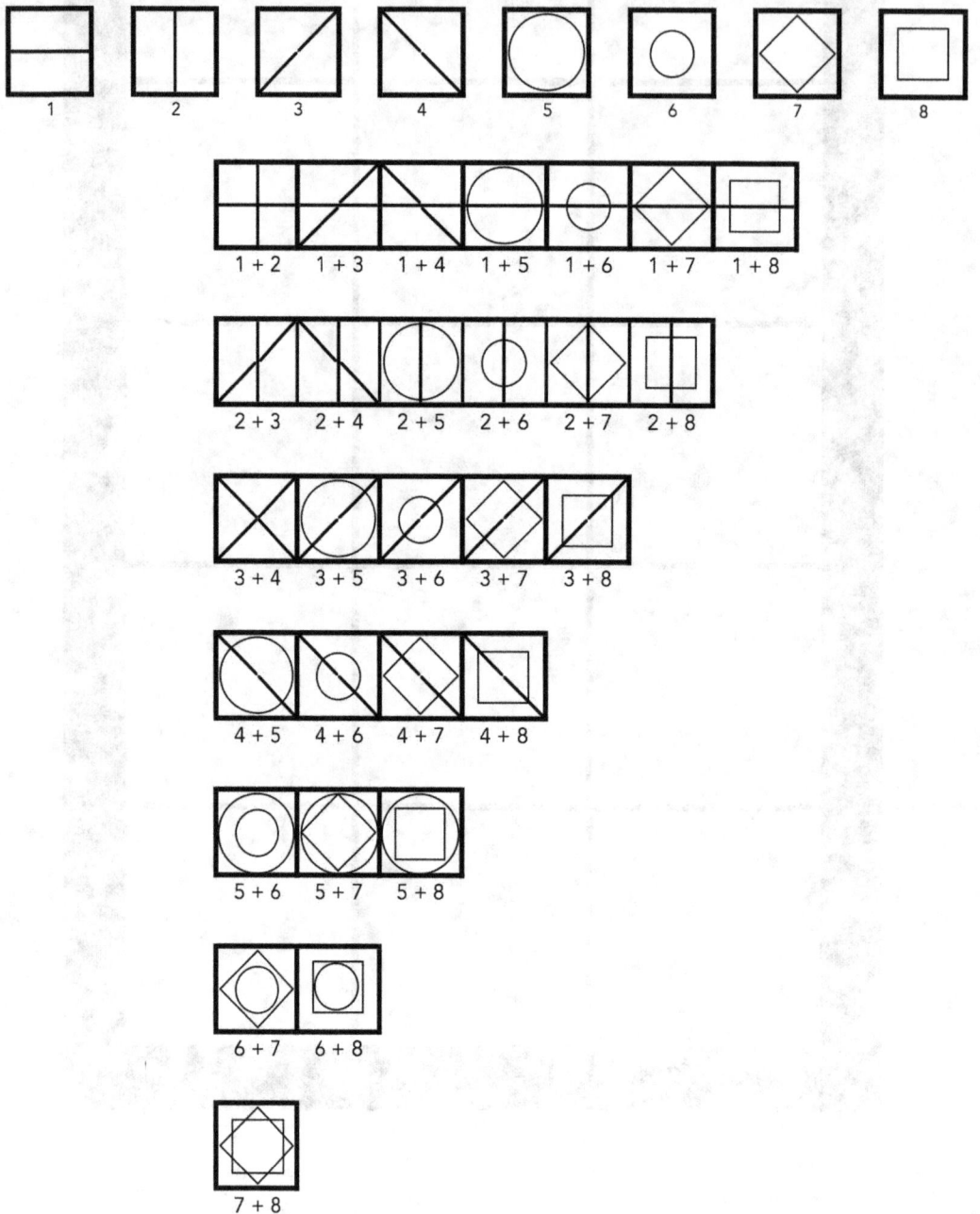

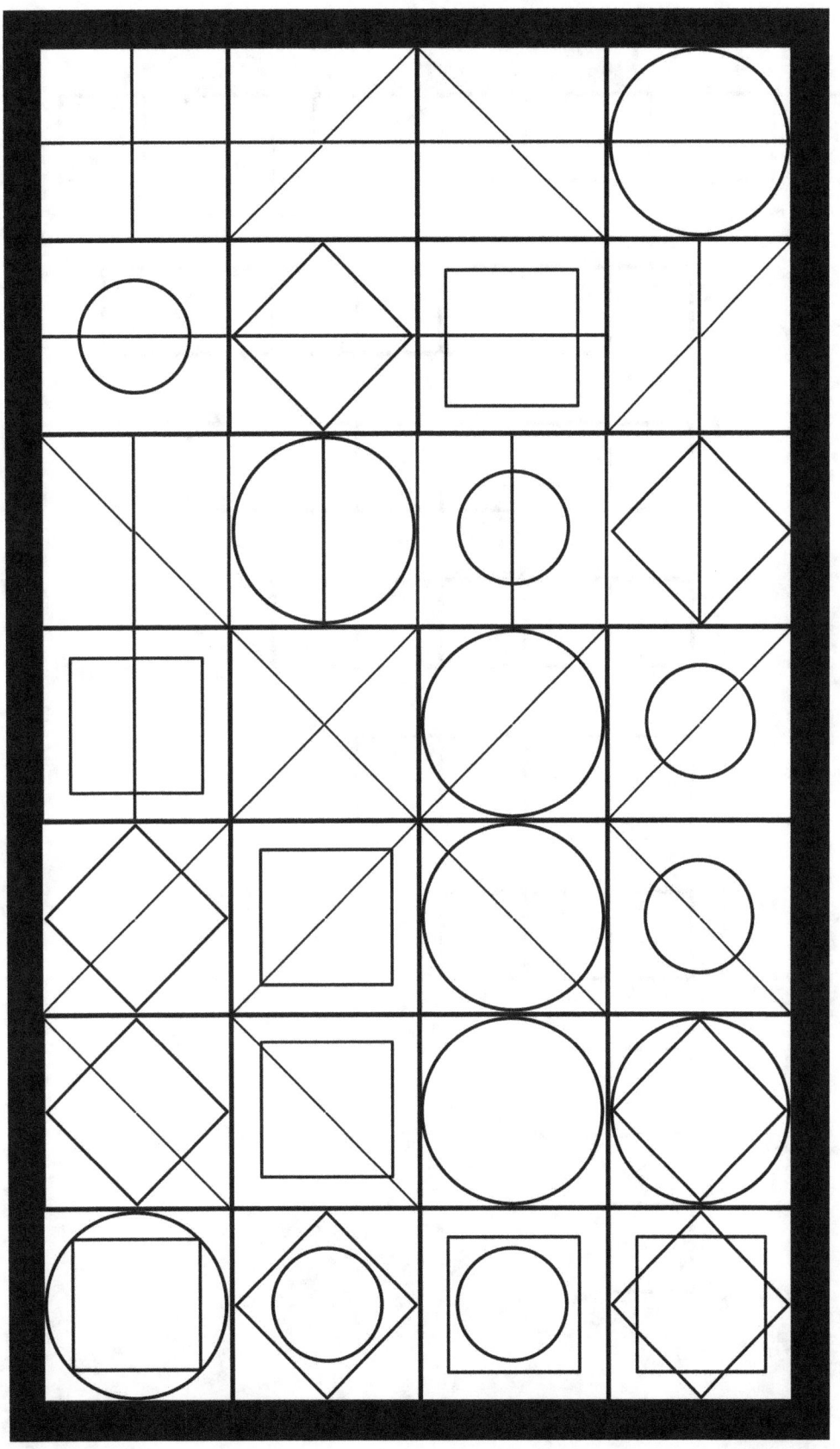

8 ELEMENTS - COMBINED TWO AT A TIME

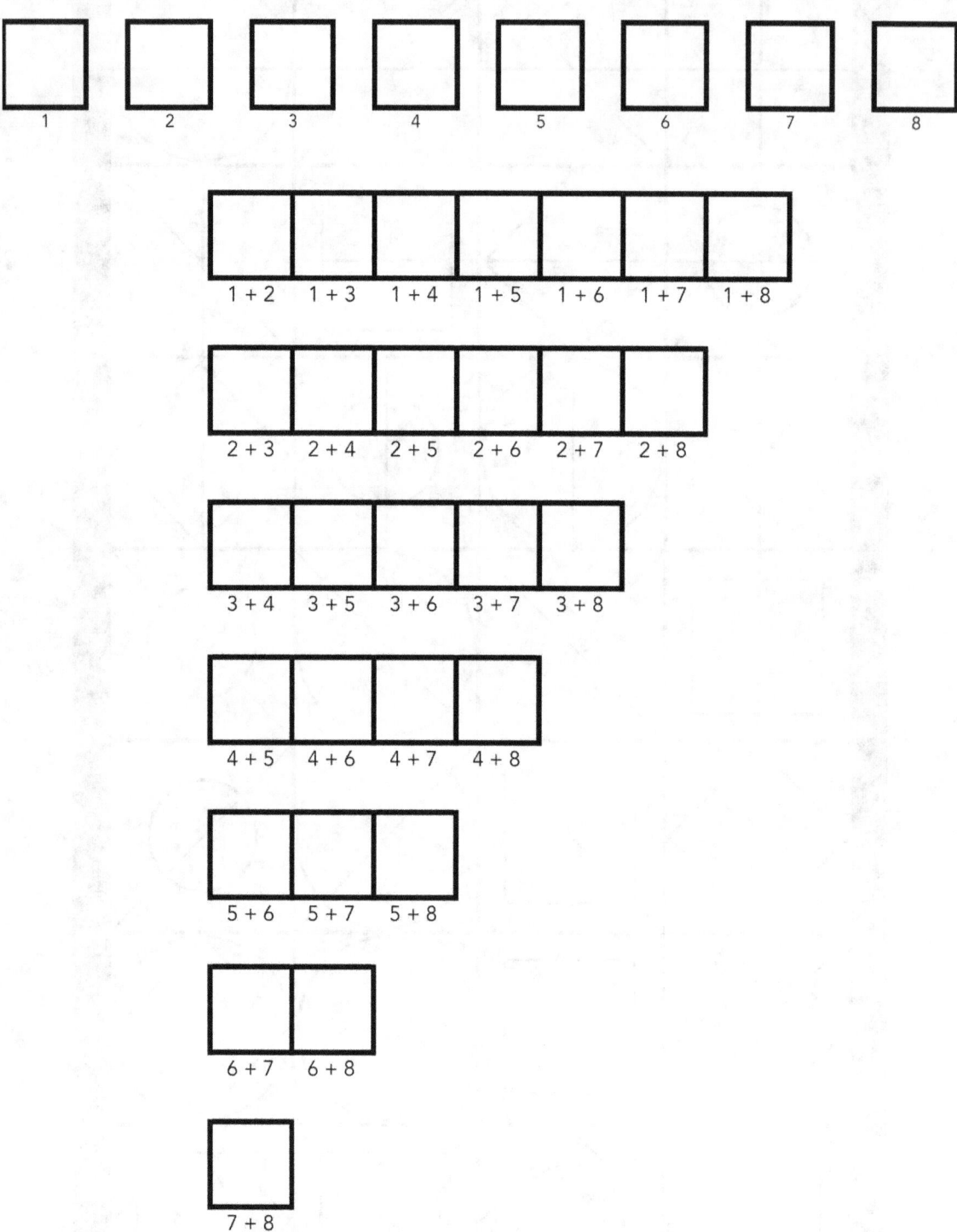